The Sorry Flowers

Also by Julia Wendell

An Otherwise Perfect History (Ithaca House Press, 1988)

Fires at Yellowstone (Bacchae Press, 1993)

Wheeler Lane (Igneus Press, 1998)

Scared Money Never Wins (Finishing Line Press, 2004)

Dark Track (WordTech Editions, 2005)

Restalrig (Finishing Line Press, 2007)

Finding My Distance (Galileo Books, 2009)

The Sorry Flowers

Poems by Julia Wendell

WordTech Editions

Published by WordTech Editions
P.O. Box 541106
Cincinnati, OH 45254-1106

ISBN: 9781934999769
LCCN: 2009940882

Poetry Editor: Kevin Walzer
Business Editor: Lori Jareo

Cover design by Charles Casey Martin

Visit us on the web at www.wordtechweb.com

In memory of my parents,
Marian Logan Wendell
and
John Potts Wendell, Sr.

And for Barrett

Acknowledgments

"In Haste"—*Spillway*

"When I Won't Take Down the Christmas Lights," "We Can't Go Back"—*"RE:AL"*

"The Shower Cap," "Good Wife" (originally titled "The Undertaker's Wife"), "Poem," "The Getaway" (originally titled "Vacationing")—*Prairie Schooner*

"Myrrah"—*Southern Poetry Review*

"Esperanza" (originally titled "Blue Moon"), "Dancing with Strangers" (originally titled "The Art Project")—*Willow Review*

"In Bed"—*Nightsun*

"Something With Diamonds in It"—*Confrontation*

"Magic Lantern"—*South Carolina Review*

"White Silence"—*Westview*

"The Woman Who Erases Things"—*Blue Line*

"Why I Love to Drink"—*Southern Indiana Review*

"Ghosts," "False Spring"—*Harford Poetry & Literary Society Review*

"After the Operation"—*Mid-America Review*

"Counting Sheep"—*Poem*

"Clocks Back"—*Meridian Anthology of Contemporary Poetry*

"Menopause," "Night Check"—*The Cimarron Review*

"World Without End"—*Wisconsin Review*

"No Reprieve"—*Permafrost*

"Weightlifter Dancing," "Blue Stuff"—*Nebraska Review*

"White Silence" (originally titled "Pentimento")—*Westview*

Table of Contents

It is far more difficult to be simple than to be complicated.

—Ruskin

Night Check

"Let your suffering eyes
and your anonymous deaths
be the bridle that keeps us from straying from each other,
be the cinch that fastens us to the belly of each day."
                    —Billy Collins, "Nine Horses"

Girth, not cinch:
Cinch is what girths do, not are.
Not bridle, shank.
Bridles are for riding, for stopping & steering,
shanks for keeping horses
close to human ways
& not straying off to wander the prairie.
Forgive me, Mr. Collins,
I've earned the little I know well,
snapped many a shank on the restless one
who senses it's time to be led out to his dusky paddock.
And the other, who needs to be kicked
& slapped, prodded to standing
for the rope that will lead her out under the McIntosh tree
so she can be more easily carted away.
I've had a girth snap under me,
my body flung from the horse's back.
A shank was ripped through my fingers
by a cranky one who'd rather
gallop back to the barn than be attached to me.
Now a pointer & a middle & a ring
bend every which way,
though I still long to walk out
into the piano of each repetitive day:
the bright song of sky & hilltop
& horses as far as the eye can see.
I know a little about
bridles made of triple-stitched South Hall leather
& bits the color of gold, some

with starling eggs
in the center of the mouthpiece
that will encourage the rankest of mares
to bend & soften.
And I know what it feels like to leg up
my Irish one of a moonstruck night check
with ropes as reins attached to each side of the halter,
his huge sides warming my bare legs—
not a kid of 12 anymore
but a tired woman of 52 summers,
who lets the horse braille his way
through the inky shadows of the farm.
That's all—so forgive me
for knowing so little
& yet having so much.
This is my gratitude.

I.
Post & Rail

Poem

In the morning I go to wake you
but you're not sleeping,
let alone hungry.
I open the notebook,
lead you out of your stall.
You gawk at the gate,
won't bolt or eat.
You could be like this for days
& never die,
staring up into my puffy eyes
each morning
from your safe repose
on my littered desk.

To hell with you,
I'll stay at the barn,
write lines in air
& hours, in feed scoops & saddle repairs,
in the way a thousand pounds
bends around my leg at the slightest
prompting. Until daylight shrugs itself off
like an old coat, night welcomed
by hungry nickers of the living.

Foresight

Trouble rides back & forth between us
on our way to the farm,
where we find Houston's front leg dangling
at an obscene angle.

The gray passes the irretrievable
to me: pick-up sticks of bones protruding
through the shattered pastern,
blood on fence boards, on grass, blood on us.

There's a certain look in a horse's eye
when he senses his end,
the same as in my mother's glazed eyes
after the last surgery, in my husband's
after his betrayal, & in my own
after mine.

I'm holding mother all over again
as the barbiturate goes in
& the horse wobbles & sinks to his knees,
the breath slowing, her eyes fluttering shut,
my husband, the moon in the door, key in the ignition,
that explosion of tires on wet pavement.

Counting Sheep

I've got my mother's breasts & hips,
my father's hands & calves,
his easy slimness—her high-pitched voice,
his obsession for being right,
her obsession for being righter.

Two arms for his, two for hers,
I watch the boomerang
on my loft ceiling: fan blades
throwing memories at the stilled moon.

Her gift of sound, love of horses;
his, of poems & words
cantering across the history texts.
His bad stomach, her worse heart.

Her way of playing angry
fingers on invisible keys—
ta-dum, ta-dum, ta-dum—
of glaring, "Couperin, my favorite," while meaning
"Don't ever speak to me that way again."

If you ignored a problem,
would it just go away?
I read between her lines,
watched her chest move up & down,

sat by her bed & listened to her breathe:
ta-dum, ta-dum, ta-dum.

It's okay to go," I whispered, hoping
if I gave her permission
she would just go to sleep.

Rhapsody

In memory of my mother

Scotch pulls from her mother,
stamps the stall floor
when the mare turns away toward her timothy.

This one's the best in the barn—
short back, long runner's legs, good angle to the shoulder.
"Who does that?" I ask my husband

as we turn out the big mare & baby,
Scotch trotting circles around her feather duster of a tail.
Just a week old, she could run for days if she had to.

It's enough to tempt faith in lesser prophets:
someone's got to be responsible for perfection.
We pause at the gate,

arms flung over the oak board fencing,
watch how near Rhapsody's flank
the newborn stands, gallops in the séance

& shadow at her mother's side
so even the wolves who see all can't see.
She's safe in her world

as long as she stays close, which will last
a few months if she's lucky, or forty-seven years
if she's anything like me.

What I Miss

Are the long backs of afternoons
stretched out on the deck with only the company
of poplars & elms at the edge of our acres.
I would wait for the sound of you,
tires crunching gravel,
our dog's tail thumping
floorboards before he dashes out
to greet you, my emissary.

How could I know it would come to
the missing which is everything?
To a hand on a steering wheel in the Superstition Mountains
outside of Phoenix, Arizona,
rewinding the past as fast as I can
to the moment you turn to a younger me
you are just getting to know,
a bottle of Merlot open on the seat between us,
my face blazing with dry heat & new love.

Myrrha

Daughter of King Cinyras of Cyprus who had incestuous relations with
her father and was changed into a myrrh tree by the gods. Their child,
Adonis, was born from the split trunk of the tree.

They say he didn't know
who crept into his room at night,
lay down beside him.

But how could a father not know
the scent of his daughter
or the shape of her hand in darkness?
Myrrha, how do I read your steady weeping?

Silenced as a homely tree, your truth
lies rooted to the split trunk,
its resin reaching far
into the familiar
when I turn in my restless sheets

to find what's
waiting for me there:
musk of bark chips
scattered in my hair
each time I take
what I shouldn't have.

The Woman Who Erases Things

Think of the color of exhaustion,
of ash, or surrender,
air that won't stir its leaves,
color of the moon on a loveless night,
staleness of a house unlived in for a while;
you enter & let the hues drift in.
Sunday afternoons with nothing in particular to do—
no mail today. From your window, the face
of a building, the face
of rain, cold tea staining its white cup,
book finished, dishes stacked,
children gone with him for the day.
The color of no turning back,
of the words, "I don't care anymore,"
a face draining to stillness
on the operating room table.
Canvas without paint, a story without words,
a taxicab with no place to go.

In sleep, you erased the yellow hat & red suitcase by the door,
the cockatiel squawking from his bronze cage,
the letter you've been meaning to open—
its dark scrabble of words—
blossom of blood on morning sheets,
even the pink begonias splayed outside your office door—
you erased it all before the stars surrendered
& the pale sun dragged itself out of bed
one more time. Would you ever get it right,
a blankness so vast it has no name,
a whiteness drained of color by all the colors
that it's made of? So much flatness
to chronicle & name before the giving up & starting over,
before the last ellipsis, or the window's edge of paper
you stare through now . . .

Weightlifter Dancing

Facing the mirror, he raises the flaps
   of his weighted arms, assays the veins
in his neck, throbbing with exertion,
   the swell of his crotch through black spandex shorts.
Then Fats Waller interrupts his concentration.
   It's the radio that diverts him
as he springs from the machine, feet tapping as he twirls,
   & the weightlifter is momentarily dancing.

Slicking back his thinning hair
   he straps himself in again.
Count to four, slowly. Grimace, then release.
   The accomplished weights collapse
onto others only dreamed of.
   Et Voila! He is that much stronger.

Coincidental partners on the Lifecycles,
   he leans toward me, panting,
"Do you like to dance?"
   And though I'm one of who-knows-how-many others
who admits to having two left feet,
   I see his body is svelte for forty-two,

divorces, kids whom he rarely sees.
   He tells me that he works the graveyard shift at Black & Decker
on a hair dryer assembly line
   & ends his day at the gym
every morning after work,
   & that he swing dances Saturdays downtown.

My muscles aching in the aftermath
   of exertion, I wonder
at this crazy art of the body,

    sculpted in sweat, only an end in itself
for me; & for him, I imagine,

for the nights he'll glance up at the glass ball
    twirling in the middle of the Rotary Club dance floor,
to see thousands of himself
    swinging from hip to hip
a girl looking something like me.

Good Wife

I watch them come & go,
black backs & umbrellas
in the rain, a lugubrious stream
that moves like water in the bleak river.
So many wives I've seen lean against

some tense relative, who stubs
out his Camel on the sidewalk,
her new grief like an overstuffed
change purse splitting open,
coins falling helter-skelter
on the funeral home drive.
My husband at the door,
"Would you care to stay with him
  a little longer, Mrs. Rose?"

And his assumed gestures of caring
call her back.
Though they won't retrieve
the young sons, heads down, racing
from the home, from their fathers
stretched out inside.
What can a person do
to ease another?

Each night,
with the sun pulled from its sky,
his weary steps at the door, &
the smell of formaldehyde & rosewater
on his lips, he kisses the lips
that belong to the face,
that belongs to the body that is mine.

When our little Stefanie was sick
those three long winter months,
he would visit her nightly,
reeking of unearthly perfume,
bearing gifts, an artful magi:

little pink soaps in the shape of hearts,
glass unicorns, books about horses
& young love. Dear God,
in the auburn light, he would bend
over the bedclothes
to kiss our daughter,
& I would shudder,
I would have to turn away.

Nights, as his hands move over my body,
I imagine the day they will move
in a different way:

to arrange my hair for
forever; to dress me
in the scarlet gown
he so admires, the one
I've never worn,
before the needle goes in,
& the cool blue fluid
runs out.

Wheeler Lane

I had a house I treated badly.
I tacked a glass porch onto its side
that overheated in the summer & got frosty
in the cooler months.

I took no interest in its garden.
I dug up the earth
& put a pool by its side. I
lived in my world, obsessed with
the pronoun "I,"
& it felt left out.

Its rooms were bright & spacious.
It raised my children & my young
adulthood, then turned to other interests,
surrounding itself
with beautiful things: azaleas & dogwoods,

rhododendrons & raspberry bushes
plus a grandfather wisteria vine
that shimmied up the railing of the front deck.
By the time I wanted out,

neither of us cared.
The damage of indifference
had already been done.
It was just a house, after all,
it could easily be left.

Twelve years, & still I wake up drenched
from the packing I can't seem to finish,
in the house I can't clear out.

I left so many things behind
in that space of regret & loss,
that ghost on Wheeler Lane.

II.
Blue Moon

Dear Stranger
extant in memory by the blue Juniata,
these letters
across space I guess
will be all we will know of one another.

So little of what one is threads itself through the eye
of empty space.

Never mind.
The self is the least of it.
Let our scars fall in love.

—Galway Kinnell, The Book of Nightmares

At the White Horse

—after Dylan Thomas

He looks out from the book,
eyes widening to take me in,
daring me to join him at the bar
or at least resist the wholeness I'd create
if only these were excised from my life—
Camels, marijuana, Anapamu.
Won't you join me in my insurrection?
Clean shaven in a ramrod suit & tie,
sporting a cigarette & Irish coffee
as if suave control were his middle name.
Though the caption reads
that at the bar on this very page
he slipped into an alcoholic coma
& died just a few months later.
I put down the book.
Surely denial is the first step
toward self-knowledge
when it's called denial.
Surely I'm not that far gone,
longing for the alarm clock
of ice ratcheting in its infinite tumbler.

Angel of Sadness

How many times have I brushed past you
in the upstairs hallway, glimpsed a fragment of wing
fluttering in the bathroom mirror?

You were there at my mother's bedside
when I was born sideways,
that was you holding the door open

for lost love, miscarriage, divorce.
How long have I given in
to your languorous darkness,

or tried to talk my way out of you
to crossed legs, pen & pad, pointed questions?
I don't know where you come from,

& I don't know who told you to come.
But you're the one
I can't seem to dance without,

swirling me up steps to a sacristy
behind whose locked door
the angel of happiness lies in state.

Spring Cleaning

She couldn't stop throwing things out.
First, the this's & that's
her husband would not even notice:
old bras & panties,
buttons & bobby pins,
cans of okra & baked beans.

Her lens homed in
on stray packs of condoms, mooshed tubes of toothpaste,
china cups, slightly chipped on their rims,
a scrabble board missing its vowels.

Couples gone single:
one candlestick, one earring, a three-fingered glove,
a single darned sock,
one rubbery shoe.

She made one complete pass
from attic to basement,
then started all over again.
The designer tags her mother had chosen,
too loose when she looked
in her elegant floor-length mirror.

Parts of her functional world were next:
things for holding & measuring:
bathroom scales, adding machine,
the silver decanter & some of the silver.
Then even that floor-length mirror.

Noise was easy:
the telephone & stereo & especially the TV
set curbside one rainy day for Good Will.

On the third or fourth pass
a delicious silence was hers.

When she turned to the essentials
she knew she was on
an irreversible roll:
tampons & washcloths,
beds & plates,
the credit cards they lived on,
the pens & computer
that made up her mind,
the half-eaten bottles of Prozac.

Coins, first foreign mementos,
Europe, pre-euro, tossed in a bowl,
then jar upon jar
of pennies & dimes.

Things others had saved
were next on her list:
her grandmother's shower cap, for instance.
Things that reminded her
of what she couldn't hold onto:
photos & love letters,
beginnings of poems,
stale & spent.

Even her bookshelves
went Spartan & bare. She kept Joyce,
she kept Gluck, she kept Marquez & St. John,
until the fewest words possible were left.

When she was at a loss for much else,
she tossed Bitten the cat
because of her penchant for eating too much
& not being able to stop.

She cut her long, straight, luminous hair,
chewed her nails down to the quick, went on a fast,
lost pounds she couldn't spare, even her
pubic hair had to go.

Her husband, just getting in from work,
a look of relief on his face as he noticed his wife
wasting away, thinking they could finally start over.
"At last," he said,
his coat & hat still balanced on her arm,
a single mote-filled ray of light,
slipping across the empty room, slicing them in two.
"You're next," she said,
handing them back.

The Getaway

2 AM

Caitlin runs into my room to wake me—
a fire alarm is blaring from another cottage.
She's wearing her Dansko clogs, clutching
her frayed blanket—her most prized possessions,
she tells me later
when all is safe. She can't rouse
her brother or me—he, the adolescent slug,
me, the divorcee who's had too much to drink.
If I'm going to die, then let me die on vacation.
And so she's out the door
to save herself, at least.

6 AM

The yellow-breasted bird
calls for more pretzel crumbs
I'd left him on the balcony, while the swish
of a coconut palm outside my window
& the waves along the shore,
repeating their old refrain, reassure me
that nothing's wrong. Beyond all this
through Drake's Channel, an O'Day Mariner
lazes by the deep within me
where the glasses of Chardonnay I drank for dinner
have long since finished their mean lullaby.
I pull the cool white sheet over my head.
Let me burn.

Rose of Jericho

*Maybe everyone had a Rose of Jericho hidden somewhere, Jack
thought. Perhaps it wasn't always the kind of tattoo you could
see, but another kind—like a free tattoo. No less a mark for life,
just one not visible on the skin.* —John Irving

I never wanted a tattoo
until I realized I already had one
hidden just under my panty line—
a bud opening its small fist
to reveal a fluttery secret at its core—

probably a lot like yours—
a scar that sealed up
everything I've never said,
that fifty years of hiding
prevent me from describing
any further to you now.

Why I Love to Drink

Driving through a suddenness
of March snow, listening to a radio talk

show about parents who let their children
drink at home, I winced, kept driving,

loving the snow, the feel
of the road in the snow.

I grew up drinking because my parents drank.
Wine with dinner, Mother insisted,

pouring her fourth, turning her cheek
the other way if I mixed a little rum

with my juice, said nothing about
my sloe gin & cranberry cruises

behind the high school football field.
They pretended not to know, hoped

if problems weren't addressed
they would just go away. Over time,

my compulsion to tell the truth
became as strong as my compulsion to conceal.

Not a day goes by I don't at least think
about having a drink, in passing throughout

the afternoon, as others long for their children.
My mouth waters as I glance at my watch,

craving after a long day the first cool sips
of Anapamu, the color of figs, the first

dialed-up sensation as the smoothness
slips down the chute of my throat,

& with it all the day's
anxieties & glitches.

My daughter looks away,
my son wants a sip.

For a few sweet moments
until the duller repetitions

of the second drink set in,
I am swallowing the world.

Esperanza

We trudged up the back ridge
to watch the blue moon rise
until we were run off by lightning flashes,
bright threats that came to nothing.
Later, from the quiet of our patio,
fireflies came & went,
a syncopated chorus
of light & hesitation.

I only know a little about love,
how it comes & goes,
then once in a blue moon
gives us another chance,
a fullness rising
somewhere behind the shepherding clouds
& the blueness of our waiting.

Addictions

1.

You were poised
when I was born
between my mother's tortured legs,
to catch me, impatient
to impress your thumbprint
on my soft, misshapen head.

From then on, everything was yours:
the spotted pony with the crooked foot,
the half-drowned insects I couldn't resurrect,
that brother who touched me,
those mother's legs made veined
& swollen by my birth, they were yours.
The sun, the moon, the first love
who never loved back,
the gift that turned my sadness
into words, they were all yours.

2.

I get Celexa from my internist now
because he won't ask why
I don't care to be touched,
& am able to keep weight like a jockey
though I'm 46 & eat like a horse.
Like the horses outside my window
that, all night & day, snip the element
that's composed mostly of water.
The pressure is on:
consume enough salad
to support a thousand pounds.
Dr. X zips into the examining
room, pats my knee, rotates

his small head on its massive
axis, dares to call me "Jule."
I'd guess his happiness of choice
is Nardil. I'm yearning for the turn
that will lift me,
like first light rimming the dark,
lifting the field outside my window
into being.

3.

When I wake, I wake in blankness:
my padded personality, chemicals on synapses,
my poetry lost in cyberspace, lodged
between the Adult Sites
& J. Crew Clearance Sales.
When it's easy to feel happy,
it's hard to say no, hard not to pop
the Lithium along with the vitamin B,
harder still
to choose art over contentment.

4.

My daughter has instructed me
to come quick:
Fuzzy's caught a bat.
I bend down
to the delicate features
of something so familiarly
wrong, one cellophane of wing,
bent back under the otherwise perfect body,
the tiny fang-filled cavern
lunging viciously at me,
& the deep, hollow, resonant
meow of our triumphant cat
rubbing my bare ankles.
The next day, the barn clock falls

to reveal another bat hanging
upside down, & on the third day,
Caitlin's pony crushes the wings
of yet another on the floor of his stall—
this sudden return to the dark,
clarified air, the balm
of stroking my fears
fluttering, transparent now. All night
through our window left ajar,
we hear the mastication
of tiny bones.

5.

Ginseng, bee pollen, antioxidants, Advil,
occasionally a vitamin B
before starting in on the wine
& popcorn. My nights
are rationed carefully.
Unless the excuse is large—
a horse with a broken bone, bad news
in the mail,
or forgetting to take the Celexa.
Then another night of heavy wine
& the clogged feeling next day,
trading pain for misery.

6.

The dull thrumming in my head begins,
the parched mouth, the panic
that has no home,
& you're knocking on my door
without your clothes on,
your body dark & slithery & reminiscent
of my first attachment to you.
I have no excuse
except a human one

& cannot turn away.
I put you in my mouth, & pull,
then sink my teeth in.

7.

Foggy headed & hung over,
I set out on a hack, crossing the stream
where a stubborn pony named Vermeer
once got caught in barbed wire
that was lurking in the brambles
when he reared back
rather than cross.
We worked for hours to free him,
as the barbs dug into his legs.
I imagine the wire still there
among the caverns of poison ivy & cattails
as I cross carefully on a horse
who's eager to feel the coolness
cleansing his sorenesses & mine
as we stand in the canopy
of shadows & the beeches
leaning into us,
lifting our heads to listen
to the stillness,
time falling randomly around us
with only an echo of the world.

How Things Fall

—For Matthew

I'd drink away the nights
at Dave's Bar in Iowa City
with a man who'd rip my fishnet stockings with his teeth
while my lover downed shots of Jameson's
egging him on from an adjacent barstool.

We caught the newscast of John Lennon's killing
on a small screen perched high
in a corner above the pool table.
We wept, felt so wronged
from our hazy world of smokes & beers,

went on drinking, our own clipped desires
too easy to confuse with the world's.
Once, he arrived on our doorstep
in a blizzard,
& we took him into our bed,

my lover & I, & loved him warm again.
Twenty years of happy hours
gone by, I hear from him while squinting
between florescent lines, hungover
from last night's fingers of Cabernet.

Still drawn to what lingers
but doesn't last, I'm savoring
the twisted paths, the burnt
touch of a friend who once
lost his flight jacket to a blizzard,

then leaned against the shower stall
as I crossed arms over my soapy breasts.
Or the other one I eventually lost,

the three of us suspended over desire
on the rope between ecstasy & anger,

which I've learned is how things usually fall.

III.
Gravity's Patients

There was a merchant in Baghdad who sent his servant to market to buy provisions and in a little while the servant came back, white and trembling, and said, Master, just now when I was in the market-place I was jostled by a woman in the crowd and when I turned I saw it was Death that jostled me. She looked at me and made a threatening gesture; now, lend me your horse, and I will ride away from this city and avoid my fate. I will go to Samarra and there Death will not find me. The merchant lent him his horse, and the servant mounted it, and he dug his spurs in its flanks and as fast as the horse could gallop he went. Then the merchant went down to the market-place and he saw me standing in the crowd and he came to me and said, Why did you make a threatening gesture to my servant when you saw him this morning? That was not a threatening gesture, I said, it was only a start of surprise. I was astonished to see him in Baghdad, for I had an appointment with him tonight in Samarra.
—Somerset Maugham

Choices

Gregory asks if he should shoot the sparrows
in the mare barn, too—tear down the clay nests
fastened to the door runners.
I have nothing against these birds
that do no damage over here.

I've asked him, however, to shoot at will
the birds that have infiltrated the insulation
in the arena barn, tearing it out in globs,
causing thousands of dollars of damage,
as well as shitting all over the barn, dive-bombing

horses & humans, with Hitchcock as their inspiration.
We hoist Gregory up in the tractor bucket
to bash the nests of eggs & baby birds.
Meanwhile, a noise box squawks
high-pitched versions of the sparrows' predators:
starlings, crows, blue jays, even monkeys.

The actuals become manic,
attacking each other, swooping down
from the rafters, scaring up clouds
of loose insulation that rain down
on humans & rile up the horses,
before escaping through barn doors into the wide

& much more silent night.
For weeks we keep ear-plugged
until the smartest figure out the ruse
& fly back into the racket
to nest once more in the luscious insulation.

Too soon again I hear the chirpings of newborns
tucked high up behind steel beams.

I ask Gregory to go fetch the BB gun
& have another go at nonexistence.

"The babies are flying," he says one morning,
surprising me in the calm of the mare barn,
looking up to the nests I've allowed to exist
where tiny dinosaurs are bursting from the seams

of overstuffed pastry,
lifting & ruffling their downy wings.
That's when Gravity looks up,
says, *It's now or never,*
& coaxes them over the edge.

White Silence

The dog comes back from a prowl
wiggling & wagging
with her new-found trophy:
a head in her mouth.

There's not much left—
a matted patch of tabby, small, white
triangular ears, just enough
to know it's ours,

so we can stop
filling in the blanks
of a better outcome.
Not knowing

is an open door
through which
anything can pass.
I want to tell the kids

that farms are hard on cats.
This looks like
fox's work.
I want to tell them

the worst in nature
can be a good thing.
But I don't.
I throw it away and I don't.

Magic Lantern

—For my father, on his eightieth birthday

I have seen the moment of my greatness flicker.
                            —T.S. Eliot

We settled into Barcaloungers,
the lights dimming to younger versions of ourselves
broadcast on the backlit study wall,
the nerves of our various passages
converted to one common shadow.

You'd man the projector
with its platter-sized tape that was endlessly
rerolled & spliced. Playing it again meant more damage,
a little else lost from our pasts with each telltale stench
of burning film, stuck

image, our cumulative groans,
someone scrambling for the light switch,
which just might save me at five in my sizzling tutu,
aboard Big Horse, or captured in the rose garden,
curtseying to the camera, before splotching to nothing.

Once, after a dinner ranging from martinis to Merlot,
you pressed to show us something old made new:
the light that was left of our childhoods converted to video.
We huddled around the TV, track lights left blaring
to watch black & white mother's fidgety ride in a surrey

with our long-dead grandmother & uncle,
the leap to a 7-year-old me,
clutching a prized pet lop-ear, Stephen
in a fringed cowboy jacket, lurching at the lens' edge,
John diving over & over into a technicolor swimming pool,

the images first quavering then brought into focus
by perfectly preserved videography.
In the TV's sure screen, I missed the screwed-up smells,
the murky yellow fog & tick-tick-ticking
of the old projector, your countless tries to get it right
in the sputtering darkness of the study
where we hunkered down & our old selves flourished.
With one touch of the remote,
you could leave us now
& it wouldn't even matter.

What Is It?

It squeaks all night, begging for silence.
The kitten has not yet discovered how to kill,
& we are poor teachers.

We try to snatch it with a sock,
but its pain eludes us.
It scuttles behind the headboard,

behind the empty suitcase & years
of dust balls & other un-doings.

Pain can find anyone's
morning, or bed. It even lights on

the word *please* when I find it
trapped on the carpet
in a circle of sunlight

& call you up from your day just beginning
to face the feeling that whatever you do
won't be enough.

Please come get.
Please don't touch. Please because
I once loved another more.

You bend to the ebbing heartbeat
as if to a philosopher's stone,
learning what can be gotten rid of

so easily for me.

After the Operation

She looks at her hands
as if wondering what
they might be called,
not with the wonder with which
a baby studies a fist
but with a bewilderment
the weight of years
tells her she should know
but is unable to summon,
as we sense what she can't
quite come back from
anymore than we
could retreat into her body
the moment we were born.

"Cats! I see cats!" she says,
climbing the walls,
hiding under the white
curtains, behind the nurses' ankles.
We're so glad she's found
the word for what she sees,
we don't care what she sees.

No Reprieve

As my mother
lies in a cloud of oxygen
three hundred miles away,

it rains & pelts & pounds
with no sign of the haybines
& their blessed churning.

We wait, while rain bends
our orchard grass & timothy,
overburdened by too much of a good thing.

The field sinks & blurs.
And still we wait, as the grass
struggles for light & nitrogen

& the rain writes its ecstatic prose
against the panes.
We try to skirt sure death long distance.

She is waiting, too.
She is told to eat,
to ask for eggs & morphine, toast & morphine,

to prepare for the mystery—
no holding back, now
that the rows have been made

& the rains have come to cover them.
There's nothing left to salvage
except to rake them thoroughly,

so the next lesser cut can grow.

Menopause

I'm poised at the podium,
but the words won't come.
My mother lies in her casket in the next room,
having been exhumed, just for the occasion.
Her fingers are pried open, arms splayed
above her head, as in the Sun Salutation
I just learned in beginning Yoga.

I'm skimming my book of poems,
not finding one I can stomach to read—
such big words & so little to say—
my gum-chewing, yawning audience
squirming in their seats.
"The child is mother of us all," I blurt,

clasping my throat,
sweat streaming, the sheets
limp & sour with myself
for the seventh day in a row.
"You've got to stop reading books like that,"
my husband advises.

I'm reopening the gift of dream
that shatters a six-month silence,

59

throwing back wet covers,
scouring the house for pen & pad.

"The worst I've ever had," I say, shaking off sleep.
He's referring to *Miracle in the Andes*,
skulls & bones scattered in the urine-soaked snow,
ghosts spilling out of the belly of the fuselage,
hooding their seared eyes, looking up
into the cruel sunshine of the Cordillera.

Forty Times in Twenty Years

He'd pull up to the house
in his turquoise Ford sedan, would never say a word
about the same frayed Mazurka I'd left out on the rack,
the growing number of knickknacks perched
on the piano's hood—

African masks, statuettes from Costa Rica,
hand-painted bowls & candelabras from Belize—
not the least perturbed that the dear instrument
had become another piece of furniture.
Paling & arthritic,

he'd pluck open his black bag,
pile the ornaments on the sofa,
prop the hood up, & get down to the tedious business
of fine-tuning. His daughter
called last week

to tell me that her father was retiring & her son
taking over the business.
According to her father's
meticulous records, it had been over a year
since my Yamaha'd been tuned.

A lot can happen in a year.
"He's got pancreatic cancer,"
the grandson tells me, as I enter into his dirge—
the same note struck
until he hears no vibrations

in the one true tone—before moving on
to the next one. Eighty-eight in all. There'll be no peace
this painstaking afternoon, as the younger

greener version takes a little longer
with each wobbly string.

"I dropped out of college
when my grandpa got sick," & adds
"Yours is the most beautiful sound
I've ever worked on," dropping clear blue eyes
to a troubled A flat.

"Who plays the piano?" I turn my back again,
not admitting my lively affairs
with Chopin,
the broodier evenings with Beethoven,
waking to Scarlatti's light & air, & Bach,

clarifying everything.
"My son," I say, over-shoulder,
"though he's worked on the same piece
for—" I stop, not meaning to sound disparaging.
"I'm worried about the B flat."

So many ornery strings in a baby grand,
allowing me to wander beyond the obsessions
with the solitary notes, arriving with him
home at night,
tossing down his black bag for the day,

to play a little Schubert or Fats Waller
for his grandfather, who's stretched out
on the sofa, paler than I remember,
but proud of his grandson for assuming his own promise
to return to each piano every half a year.

The Shower Cap

For my daughter

I unfold the musty-sweet of Grandmother's Lake Chautauqua.
Churning into the bathroom mirror in my first striped two-piece,

I was all alone with her lily-scented soaps & porcelain swans
   & shower cap
as sailboats lazed on the water, just outside her very pink window.

It was a plastic cap, with little colored dots
scattered over the hood, & a terribly frayed elastic,

which, in all the world, could only have been hers.
My mother chose the signature keepsake,

then left it at the bottom of a dresser drawer for twenty years.
Each Easter, without fail, the pot of lilies would arrive

in a delivery truck chugging up the driveway.
I never had to check the card to know the sender.

No longer. Some things you can never own
but only choose & guard & then pass on,

a piece of plastic or a scent
tucked between the lines of a poem.

Angels

I remember that sinking feeling as we rose,
instructions to raise our seatbacks & lift our shades
while softer curtains parted for us,

revealing haze & more confusion,
a sky-full of white peonies
pulled inside out as we punched through.

My fear of flying at last gone:
I was on a mercy trip
& surely would be spared.

Unlike my father.
I'd come north to be his mouth, his eyes,
his will to not keep breathing.

I would lift that shade
as the air was pulled & the skin turned yellow,
lungs doing their job with no return.

I'm glad he objected at the end—
back arched, lungs gasping.
I'm glad his body said no,
each breath not willed but resurrected.

I stopped the going for him,
wanting him to stay almost as much
as I wanted him to join me

thirty thousand feet above the earth,
cotton & peonies & the rest of my life
blooming right outside the window,
gravity's patients such a long way down.

IV.
The Sorry Flowers

In Haste

Cutting back the brown perennials,
yanking the wild violet & mint
that have overrun the scalloped flowerbed—
shaping clumps of crew cuts—I hurry through
my hatred of this work

because it is never ending.
Because they always come back,
like regret. What would it take
to plant something else:
a stone wall, for instance?

Blue Stuff

It was midnight before I noticed
the swimming-pool blue of the aquarium,
the tetras & sucker fish & angels
treading the drugged water,
two dollops lying unfocused on the gravel floor.
But I'd already had a day
of feedings & scoopings & fixings,
so I made a mental note
to start here in the morning.

When two more were dead.
I spatula-ed those silver eggs
down the toilet, taking note
to wait to tell the children till they'd
gotten home from school, the navy water now,
van Gogh's Starry Night.

In an idle moment between piano
& TV, John discovered all the rest
bobbing on the surface.
Except one fat drugged angel who'd made it through
two other Armageddons of this aquarium tank.
A lot of commotion,
scooping & splashing, phoning
a long-distance father
who'd surely add this to his list
of my failures. While Caitlin stood silently by,
accounting wide-eyed for herself,
counting cupfuls of the blue stuff
she'd tossed in without asking,
only trying to be helpful.

I pulled her close
to explain the difference

between intent & accident
& simply having too much to do,
admitting that I too have put the blue stuff in
only to watch what rises, bellies up,
or clings to the thermometer,
remembering how I'd turned my own burning cheek
one too many times the other way,
the fragments of our family,
floating still life in the starry sky.

When I Won't Take Down the Christmas Lights

Then it was August & clusters
of pine cones
hung in concert or competition
from the tree, like oversized earrings
on an earring tree. I'd kept meaning to,
as one month fed another
& the seasons turned warmer,
until the taking down would seem anachronous
& foresight would be doing nothing at all. Each morning
on the way to the barn, I'd scold myself,
thinking of stuffed closets, unanswered
letters, appointments I'd meant to make.
Until every undone gesture was a bulb on that tree.
Until I wake to the film of first snow,
my stiff joints unable to recall
what the claustrophobic heat of August
even felt like——& it's time,
once again, to plug them in.

In Bed

We lounge at the table after supper
reading fortune cookies' fortunes.
My daughter's got a new trick, suggested
by her seventh-grade pal, Josie.
You will have a long & productive life
in bed. She squeals, flings it across
the table toward her brother's face,
then explains, "Add in bed
after every line." I offer mine, to play along.
Seeing is believing, but try believing first
in bed. Barrett's cookie's
had twins. He takes his pick.
Next year, all your efforts will pay off
in bed. Snickers all around
the opened paper cartons,
the spent scents of soy, mustard, sweet & sour
comingling. Son John
lunges for the rejected future
of his stepfather.
You must learn to trust the ones you love
in bed. He bellows,
refusing to read his own, darts

upstairs, fist closed around
his tiny slip of paper.
Fifteen & in first-time love,
he's not bound to share a thing.
Except endless e-mails
to Gillian, a name with a tinge
of Guinevere in it.
He sits at the keyboard
as if pulling up the covers
for the evening, reveals himself
by entering name & password,

then hears the deep, delicious
anonymous male voice
informing him that he's got mail.
In bed.

False Spring

1.

An armful of branches brought inside
I trick into thinking it's spring.
Tight buds open
to a splash of sun, tossed
from its bucket of sky

through a closed window
& onto my bookshelves.
Too hot, too fast, green tips
quiver & fall.

What hurry am I in
wrenching too soon into something else
what wants to be given slowly?

2.

Nothing lonelier than an iris
stranded against a garden fence.

Others of her kind, tight-fisted,
wait for warmer weather.

Not her. She volunteers
to go first,

her lesson in loss,
a frost-slip away.

3.

Dandelions infest
newly fertilized turf
just days out from its second cutting.

A cool wind creaks in,
bright white balls scattering feathers, or confetti.
I can't stop it now.

Dancing with Strangers

She hauled the art project home
in her brother's VW,
scratched the hatch paint
when she pried it out,

carted it up the stone steps
& into the mud room
of our farm house.

"We had to show movement
& light," she informed us.
"Everyone else made kaleidoscopes,
but I had my heart set on a chair."

She hammered for hours in her art class
the seat of the old metal stool
where she glimpsed
splintered versions of herself.

"Downright dangerous," we joked
around the dinner table,
wincing at the shards
of mirror glued on top

of our dented images,
concertina wire
wound helter-skelter
around the stainless legs

until we imagined
a kind of movement there,
a two-step forming
at the edge of our minds,

a debutante in her stiff
hoop skirt swooping
over a gleaming dance floor
& balanced on the arm

of some tantalizing stranger.

Back & Forth

The glads have given up on me—
I should have cut them days ago.

In the early morning's opaque tang—
waning cicadas & autumn-cool—
I walk by an open upstairs
window, & there I am again:

the mint-rich pleasure of boxwood
drifting through the brittle
screen, mallards paddling across
Grandmother's pond, the tennis court's
green tuftings through asphalt.

And my father's pony
pawing for his morning grain
in the bank barn that will cave
in on itself from the weight

of everything that has happened to it
since 1926 . . . the tall
spikes of gladioli
coloring in the outlines

of the broken fence
& broken barn.
My father is a boy
about to wake
in a room since crammed with

box after box of
the pushed aside & missing
that years later
I poke through,

a girl in love
with useless boxes & rooms.
Impatient for him to wake, grow up,
then engender me,

I snip the withered spikes
of the neglected flowers
before the sun ruins them
beyond remembering.

John

As a child I'd ask to see
your grandfather's bear claw,
would he please turn it over
so I could trace Alaska on his palm?

He'd rotate the much larger
version of my own
to show the contour of his flaw,
a red, angry birthmark I was miffed

not to have myself.
I would reach to touch that state,
but he would close the fist,
put a glove back on. Too cold.

Mornings, when I go into your room,
Give me a foot, I say,
which emerges like a turtle's head
from under the warm shell of sheets.

I pull each long, slender toe, both of us hoping
for that satisfying snap. Give me the other,
noting the dime-sized freckle
stamped in one drowsy curve, grateful
for your uninhibited scars, your very bones.

Ghosts

Bodiless they hang,
       upside down,
like deflated scarecrows waiting to be filled.
Until a wind comes along
& lifts them into form,
       & I see
the stout plaid farmer squatting like a toad
on his Massey Ferguson,
his plump floral wife leaning against
her spade, having,
       for the infinite time,
chinked out the stiff spring earth
of her windswept garden.
I wish it were as easy as
waiting for the next gust
       to come along
to be caught up & solidified.
Get me down from here,
I imagine them pleading to the wind,
tethered as they are to this world
by the immaculately smooth,
       flesh-colored
clothespins.

Something With Diamonds in It

I'm looking out my family-room window
        when I see a man I don't know,
bare chested & barefoot, a towel around his loins,
        scooting out the back door.

First coffee cup in hand,
        I blink & look again.
From inside, my daughter's turned the knob,
        looking furtive over a shoulder, as if for me.

She's back from six weeks in The Village,
        preferring time with a father
I don't know anymore.
        Next, two more boys

race out the front door toward their jalopies.
        Scanning the driveway,
I count twelve more cars.
        I'm as ashamed as I am miffed.

Should I punish
        or choose something with diamonds in it,
the glitter of kindness?
        What's her secret?—

questions I no more know how to answer
        than I know how to end this
one night stand under the starry roof
        of my imagination,

except to strip it, wrap a towel around,
        & scoot it out the back door
with all the others.

The Sorry Flowers

Like old men snoozing, heads
drooping on their stems,
my week-old dozen roses
won't go anywhere I want them to.
They won't get up from this couch
& run a mile; they won't stop
at the drug store, or even throw themselves away.
Because they're the sorry flowers—
their yellow the color of sympathy, not love,
escorting Our Deepest Regret
on the death of your friend, your
father, the loss of a job,
& this time, my broken ankle—
minor, to be sure, in the scope of what's to come.
Though cheering is what they're meant
to do, I lie on the couch all day,
watch stones drop
from the crumbling velvet center of each rose.

17

Pushing uneaten
crumbs around on our plates,
it just slips out. I hadn't meant to say it.
I was talking about her actual birth-
day, how late she was,

how I'd asked the doctor
to break the sack
though labor had already stopped.

So comes
news of the other,
& something of the mother's will,
how we get here, or don't,
the luck, the decisions, the sheer hard work.

And the shapes we see
at the farthest edge, the blur
of hands.

Her chocolate eyes grow huge.
I hope she is old enough
& has the tools
to judge me well.

The cake is dry,
the marshmallow icing
hardened to glue.
I am a good cook, usually,
& she knows it.

Music Lessons

She grew up with music
& now lives just about without it:
CD cases scattered throughout the house
emptied by her careless young,
unfamiliar hits on the radio
she flicks to from time to time.

All day, every day, the Bose played its Brahms,
its Beethoven, its schmaltzy Rachmaninoff
in the elevator of her parents' house.
She hated this predictability
as she hated her own self-consciousness:
too tall, too fat, too many pimples on her face. . .
she could never turn it off.

"He's into music," she'd say to her mother
to convince her of a new beau's worth,
thinking of his Hendricks, his Dylan, his Jerry Garcia.
"But does he like *good* music?" her mother would reply,
always with the twist of the next question
involving The Killer B's
with a little Rameau thrown in.

She stopped practicing her scales,
did more talking & asking in her music lessons
than playing, notes of words
spilling out of her, masking
her lack of preparation.

Music took on different guises:
the breathing in & out when she was pushing
a child into the world,
counting the horse's strides to a jump,
or the syllables in a line of verse.

So that when her son asked to take music lessons,
then wanted a guitar of his own for Christmas,
she was glad to oblige,
as her dead mother's Bechstein brooded,
squat, in a corner of her living room.

Before He Goes off to College

The Lelands have quadrupled in size.
And the corner look-out bedroom
you once built for him
has lost its view of fence & field,
obscured rather than
                    illuminated now.

In the full-length mirror,
cupping sagging breasts,
your bony chest & ribcage
rise to the surface, inviting you
to look a little farther—
the cypresses razed,
the boy grown,
the lookout burnt
to a fleck
in a deeply weathered
eye.

World Without End

We'd lie out in the rose garden
nestled in our sleeping bags
dreaming of the sky, of the farthest reaches,

all the barriers & never endings
we knew. Infinity was a giant wall,
locked door, never-ending

silence, the blackness
when we first closed our eyes,
all the waitings

we waded through as children—concerts,
semesters, dinner parties, church,
the wide ocean of Sunday afternoons

& the day after Christmas—
the dull ache of nothing left
to look forward to.

On some braver nights
from our cozy sleeplessness
we eased into adolescence

by dreaming our own ends,
God waiting for us on the lip
of space beyond the last

thin star, handing us a yellow rose
to carry into our non-future.
Later, from stiff-backed

pews, we'd recite prayers
about a world we'd memorized
without end, sandwiched between

the Kyrie Eleison & the Agnus Dei—-
until we smelled again
the musk of our sex

escaping from deep under down,
smelled the American Beauties,
the Sunbursts & Tangerine Ladies,

preparing with all their loveliness
for the sharp blade
of Mother's fantastic shears.

Clocks Back

Moonlight slithers
between my window shade & sill
startling me awake,
as if some stranger had entered the room.
"What's that?" I say
to my snoring mate,
who somehow hears me,
astutely grunting, "Huh?"

"It's the moon," I say,
nudging him awake
as if I needed his confirmation
of its brightness, its
actual-ness, to be sure.

And sure enough, the sliver moon
has plenty of room
to fit quite nicely
between the two-inch space
the wood & fabric create
just above our sleigh bed,

imploring me with its loud light
to get up from my night of nothing
because everything is ready for me,
not a mere luminous
hour from now, but now.

Revealed

I happen on it
in the stillness of an early
morning, coffee & manuscript
balanced on my lap.

The color
of my velvety Christmas best,
full moon-like,
with plush, splayed folds

to rival what I imagine
of my darkest parts.
Does it need pointing out
to be true?

Does it want to be left
or brought in & admired,
hung on the wall of my coffee table?

Better to nourish from a distance—
the green dollop of hummingbird
that quivers by the flower's petals
seems to need it there.

One solitary rose
outside my window
topping a lone, tall, snaggly bush.

Thump

Each time I sit down at my desk,
the cardinal goes at it,

bashing against my windowpane
to get at the red feathers

lodged in my glass.
Stupid bird. There's no one in here but me.

Thump. Thump. Thump.

In another tale, his irresistible reflection
might be freed from the glass,

or at least move a little,
the way water moved the image of Narcissus.

Instead, my bird will thrash himself
senseless with unknowing,

programmed as he is to merge with his own likeness.
Worse than fingernails run along a chalkboard,

or my husband's snoring, far more aggravating
than my brother chewing with his mouth open.

I ask the husband to roll over,
& Brother only flies in once a year with his bad manners.

Then a silence opens up
the pane of my own flapping.

Thump. Thump.

I am nestled in a house
of stray things, hair, straw, daub

sculpted to cup us up, those fuzzy others
& myself, balanced

on a chestnut beam in the bank barn.
I am opening my mouth

to be fed whatever she brings me—
if she can escape the nasty paws

of the barn cat, sizing me up down there.
I want to eat & live & sing,

I want to fly on my new wings,
leave the barn & its longings,

leave the frustrated poet, head in hands,
lodged behind her windowpane.

I sense air & sky
& a bright-blue, immeasurable day. And life

beyond what contains us.

Julia Wendell was born and raised in Warren, Pennsylvania. She received degrees from Cornell University, Boston University and The University of Iowa Writers' Workshop. After making careers as an editor and teacher and mom, she returned her attention to her childhood passion of horses. Since 1995, she has been engaged in the sport of three-day eventing. She is the author of three full-length collections of poems and three chapbooks, plus a memoir, *Finding My Distance: A Year in the Life of a Three-Day Event Rider*. She lives in northern Baltimore County on a horse farm which she works alongside her husband, Barrett Warner.

Author photo: Hannah Ong

LaVergne, TN USA
25 February 2010
174222LV00005B/11/P